FREAKY TRUE SCIENCE

FREAKY
ANIMAL STORIES

BY MICHAEL CANFIELD

Gareth Stevens
PUBLISHING

Please visit our website, www.garethstevens.com. For a free color catalog of all our high-quality books, call toll free 1-800-542-2595 or fax 1-877-542-2596.

Library of Congress Cataloging-in-Publication Data

Canfield, Michael.
Freaky animal stories / by Michael Canfield.
p. cm. — (Freaky true science)
Includes index.
ISBN 978-1-4824-2948-0 (pbk.)
ISBN 978-1-4824-2949-7 (6 pack)
ISBN 978-1-4824-2950-3 (library binding)
1. Animals — Miscellanea — Juvenile literature. 2. Animals — Juvenile literature. I. Canfield, Michael. II. Title.
QL49.C36 2016
590—d23

First Edition

Published in 2016 by
Gareth Stevens Publishing
111 East 14th Street, Suite 349
New York, NY 10003

Copyright © 2016 Gareth Stevens Publishing

Designer: Sarah Liddell
Editor: Ryan Nagelhout

Photo credits: Cover, background throughout book andreiuc88/Shutterstock.com; cover, p. 1 (tail) AKaiser/Shutterstock.com; cover, p. 1 (wing used throughout book) Mur34/ Shutterstock.com; cover, p. 1 (snake) Life On White/Photodisc/Getty Images; pp. 5, 7, 9, 11, 13, 15, 17, 19, 21, 23, 25, 27, 29 (hand used throughout) Helena Ohman/Shutterstock.com; pp. 5, 7, 9, 11, 13, 15, 17, 19, 21, 23, 25, 27, 29 (texture throughout) Alex Gontar/ Shutterstock.com; p. 5 Keystone-France/Gamma Keystone/Getty Images; p. 7 Steven Senne/Associated Press/AP Images; p. 9 John Macgregor/Photolibrary/Getty Images; p. 11 The Asahi Shimbun Premium/Getty Images; p. 12 Krzysiu/Wikimedia Commons; p. 13 Yonatanh/Wikimedia Commons; p. 15 PEDRO UGARTE/Staff/AFP/Getty Images; p. 16 David Haring/DUPC/Iconica/Getty Images; p. 17 David Haring/DUPC/Oxford Scientific/Getty Images; p. 19 Gary Meszaros/Science Source/Getty Images; p. 21 Stew Milne/Associated Press/AP Images; p. 22 James Ambler/Barcroft Media/Getty Images; p. 23 Barcroft Media/Contributor/Getty Images; p. 25 Bob Landry/Contributor/The LIFE Picture Collection/Getty Images; p. 27 Spencer Sutton/Science Source/Getty Images; p. 29 (bottom woolly mammoth) Science Photo Library - LEONELLO CALVETTI/Brand X Pictures/Getty Images; p. 29 (paleomastodon and Gomphotherium) FunkMonk/ Wikimedia Commons; p. 29 (mastodon) Haplochromis/Wikimedia Commons; p. 29 (top mammoth) Dewaere/Wikimedia Commons; p. 29 (Asian elephant) YANGCHAO/ Shutterstock.com; p. 29 (African elephant) Abbie/Shutterstock.com.

Printed in the United States of America

CPSIA compliance information: Batch #CS15GS: For further information contact Gareth Stevens, New York, New York at 1-800-542-2595.

CONTENTS

Words in the glossary appear in **bold** type
the first time they are used in the text.

ANIMALS RULE!

Animals are everywhere. We see them when we leave the house, and many of us have them in our homes as pets. They're a living, breathing part of our world and make it a lot more interesting!

We rely on animals as a source of food. We also like to study animals and figure out what makes them act as they do. Animals are full of surprises, and sometimes, the surprises are freaky. Studying animals, even the animals you don't see every day, tells us a lot about how our world works, even if it doesn't always make sense. Have you ever seen a two-faced cat? Or what about a female lion that took care of a baby antelope instead of having it for dinner?

FREAKY FACTS!

Discovering something freaky begins with someone noticing something weird and asking "why." This skill,

WHAT ARE ANIMALS?

Animals are living organisms from the group Animalia. Many familiar animals are able to move on their own as they please. They have to eat other living beings or what organisms produce, like fruits, to stay alive. Animals are broken down into several subgroups, including vertebrates, which are birds, mammals, amphibians, reptiles, and fish. There are also mollusks and arthropods, to name a few other types of animals.

WHEN SCIENTISTS DISCOVER SOMETHING
FREAKY ABOUT ANIMALS, THEY START TO
ASK QUESTIONS TO FIGURE OUT WHY.

THE STORY OF FRANKENLOUIE

Frank and Louie, or "Frankenlouie," was a cat born with two faces in Massachusetts in 1999. Although the veterinarian thought he would die soon after birth, he lived for 15 years! Frank and Louie had two mouths, two noses, two normal eyes, and a large eye that didn't work between the two faces.

According to his owner, Frank did the eating while Louie just went along with what Frank did. Early in his life, Frank and Louie's owner had to feed him a special formula through tubes in both his mouths. Much to the surprise of veterinarians familiar with him, Frank and Louie became stronger every day, living a long, high-quality life. Frank and Louie died in 2014.

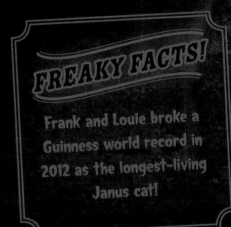

FREAKY FACTS!

Frank and Louie broke a Guinness world record in 2012 as the longest-living Janus cat!

DIPROSOPUS

Diprosopus (dy-pruh-SOH-puhs) is a rare disorder where the face, or parts of the face, are **duplicated**. Animals with the disorder, like Frank and Louie, rarely survive due to problems with their brain and internal organs. Cats with two faces are called Janus cats, named after the Roman god Janus, who had two faces. One of the most famous animals with two faces was a pig named Ditto. Diprosopus can also happen to people, although most don't live longer than a

7

POLYCEPHALY

While Frankenlouie was born with two faces, some animals are born with two or more heads! This is called polycephaly. People born with polycephaly are known as conjoined twins. The condition has been documented in animals for hundreds of years.

Just as with animals born with two faces, animals born with two or more heads face an uphill battle to survive. The heads of a polycephalic animal each contain its own brain, which shares control of the animal's organs and limbs. Polycephalic animals struggle to walk normally. It's almost as if their brains are fighting each other for control of the animal's body. The disorder is most common among snakes and frogs, but it's also seen in farm animals like sheep, pigs, and cattle and even cats and dogs!

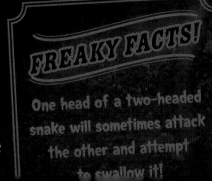

FREAKY FACTS!

One head of a two-headed snake will sometimes attack the other and attempt to swallow it!

EACH HEAD OF A TWO-HEADED ANIMAL CONTAINS A BRAIN, FIGHTING FOR CONTROL OF THE ANIMAL'S BODY.

THE FREAK SHOW

Some polycephalic animals find themselves traveling with county fairs as sideshows. The Venice Beach Freakshow claims to have the largest number of two-headed animals on display. Several museums around the world keep preserved collections of two-headed animals

MYANMAR SNUB-NOSED MONKEY

In 2010, scientists discovered a new species of monkey in Myanmar, Asia. The monkey is **endangered**. It has a turned-up nose that makes it sneeze when it rains! In fact, locals told researchers to listen for the monkeys sneezing when they were searching the forests for them. The first known photographs of the monkeys were taken in 2012.

Snub-nosed monkeys were also found in China in 2011. The monkeys stand less than 2 feet (0.6 m) tall and have mostly black fur, with some white tufts. Their faces are hairless, with the exception of a white beard and a line of white hairs above their upper lip, almost like a mustache!

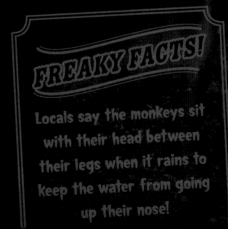

FREAKY FACTS!

Locals say the monkeys sit with their head between their legs when it rains to keep the water from going up their nose!

ENDANGERED

The Myanmar snub-nosed monkey is considered critically endangered by the International Union for **Conservation** of Nature, which is an organization working on conservation around the world. Scientists believe there are between 260 and 330 monkeys in Myanmar and fewer than 100 in China. The idea of creating a special national park to protect the monkeys in Myanmar has been explored. Hunting, logging, and isolation from other animals all contribute to the monkey's current situation.

IN 2014, MORE THAN 20 MONKEYS
WERE CAUGHT ON VIDEO
FOR THE FIRST TIME!

WENDY THE WHIPPET

Wendy is a dog with double the usual amount of muscles in her body. She weighs twice as much as a normal whippet, but acts just the same, despite her big muscles. Born in British Columbia, Canada, Wendy weighs 65 pounds (29.5 kg). Wendy's owner says she's just a normal dog who loves attention and playing with other dogs.

Wendy is actually a kind of whippet called a "bully." Bully whippets don't make a protein called myostatin in their body. Myostatin limits muscle growth. In whippets that race, picking up this **genetic mutation** from one parent increases their speed on the racetrack. For bully whippets like Wendy, who pick up the mutation from both parents, the usually slight-framed dog ends up with twice as much muscle.

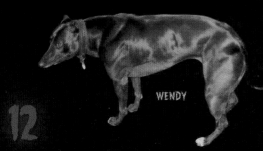

WENDY

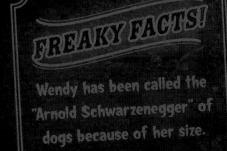

FREAKY FACTS!

Wendy has been called the "Arnold Schwarzenegger" of dogs because of her size.

SOME SCIENTISTS ARE WORKING
ON DRUGS FOR HUMANS THAT BLOCK
MYOSTATIN PRODUCTION TO HELP
PEOPLE BUILD MUSCLE.

MYOSTATIN

Whippets aren't the only animals who may lack myostatin because
of a mutation. Some livestock have been bred to have the mutation.
However, the increase in muscle creates some problems. These animals
need special care and have trouble making babies. The cost of
veterinary care and the expense of caring for the animals decreases
any benefit of extramuscular cattle for farmers. The mutation and
its effects continue to be studied in both animals and humans.

KAMUNYAK

Kamunyak was a lioness living in an African wildlife reserve. Between 2002 and 2003, Kamunyak adopted at least six baby antelopes, animals she would normally eat for dinner! The lioness watched over the young antelopes like they were her own babies.

In order to take in the baby antelopes, Kamunyak would separate them from their mothers, then fend off other predators who were interested in the babies for a meal. The first antelope rangers saw Kamunyak caring for was eaten by a male lion. Kamunyak did eventually eat one of the baby antelopes she took in, her fifth one, after it had already died. Kamunyak didn't hunt while caring for the antelopes. She seemed too worried about her baby antelopes to worry about food!

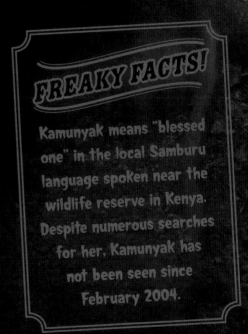

FREAKY FACTS!

Kamunyak means "blessed one" in the local Samburu language spoken near the wildlife reserve in Kenya. Despite numerous searches for her, Kamunyak has not been seen since February 2004.

MANY PEOPLE, INCLUDING SCIENTISTS, FLOCKED TO THE ANIMAL PRESERVE TO WATCH KAMUNYAK TAKE CARE OF HER BABY ANTELOPES.

FREAKY RELATIONSHIPS

Kamunyak's relationship with the baby antelopes isn't the only example of strange animal pairings in the wild. In 2012, another lioness in Queen Elizabeth National Park in Uganda adopted a baby antelope after killing and eating its mother. It took about 45 minutes for the two animals to get used to each other. While rare, **interspecies** relationships fascinate tourists and researchers alike, especially when it involves predator and prey.

15

AYE-AYES

Aye-ayes (EYE-EYEZ) are only native to the island of Madagascar, an island off the coast of Africa. While they more closely resemble rats, they're actually primates, like monkeys, apes, and people. They're **nocturnal** and find food by tapping on trees and listening for grubs under the bark. They use their teeth to make a hole in the tree and remove the grubs with their long middle fingers.

Aye-ayes spend all their time in trees and curl up in a nest of leaves and branches during the day. They rarely come down from the trees. They have large eyes, sensitive ears, and a big, bushy tail that's bigger than the rest of their body. They have a big toe on each foot that allows them to hang from branches in the rainforest.

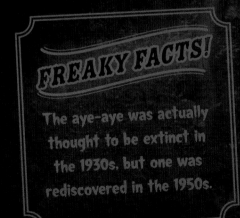

FREAKY FACTS!

The aye-aye was actually thought to be extinct in the 1930s, but one was rediscovered in the 1950s.

SUPERSTITION

Aye-ayes are considered an endangered species for several reasons. Their **habitats**, the rainforests of Madagascar, are being destroyed, and farmers kill them to protect their farmland. Locals also consider them to be evil and believe they bring bad luck, so they're often killed. The animal is also hunted by **poachers**. Madagascan schoolchildren have been trained in how to protect the animals in their native habitat.

17

STAR-NOSED MOLE

The star-nosed mole is found in the eastern part of Canada and in the northeastern United States. It's easy to spot because of its freaky face! It has 22 different parts, called appendages, around its snout that look like little pink tentacles!

These appendages are used for touching things. Each has 25,000 tiny **sensory** receptors on it. Also known as Eimer's organs, the appendages help the mole to feel its way around and find food.

The star-nosed mole is a good swimmer that feeds on water insects, small fish, mollusks, and small amphibians. The mole is active all through the winter and has even been seen swimming in frozen creeks! These freaky animals are food for hawks, owls, cats, and even some large fish.

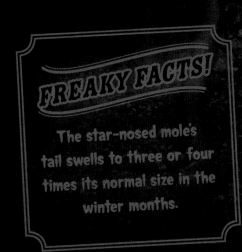

FREAKY FACTS!

The star-nosed mole's tail swells to three or four times its normal size in the winter months.

EIMER'S ORGANS?

Eimer's organs are sensory organs found on most moles, but most notably on the star-nosed mole. They were discovered in the 1870s by German zoologist, or animal scientist, Theodor Eimer. The mole uses its special appendages to smell underwater, something that was previously thought to be impossible for mammals!

THE STAR-NOSED MOLE USES THE APPENDAGES AROUND ITS SNOUT TO FEEL WHERE IT IS AND WHAT'S AROUND IT, EVEN PREDATORS.

THE DEATH CAT

Oscar is a cat who lives at the Steere House Nursing and Rehabilitation Center in Providence, Rhode Island. Born in 2005, Oscar was raised at the nursing home, where old and sometimes sick people live. According to some workers there, Oscar is able to sense when someone at the nursing home is going to die!

After about 6 months at the nursing home, doctors and nurses noticed Oscar making his own rounds to the patients. Oscar would choose a patient and curl up and sleep with them. The patients he chose usually died within several hours of Oscar's arrival!

No one knows for sure how Oscar knows who will die, but they have some ideas. Some think Oscar can see a patient's lack of movement or can smell something called ketones, chemicals released by a dying person.

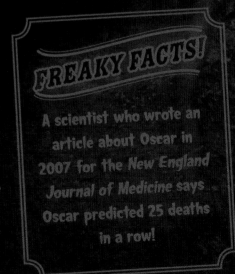

20

OSCAR HAS BEEN PREDICTING DEATH AT THE NURSING HOME HE LIVES AT FOR NEARLY A DECADE.

ACCURACY

Oscar has become so good at knowing when a patient is going to die that nursing home staff notify family members when he chooses a patient to sleep with. Most families don't mind Oscar being in the room. Those who make Oscar leave find him pacing back and forth outside the room.

DOG, THE ARTIST

A Jack Russell terrier who can draw and create art sounds like a joke, right? Well, Tillamook Cheddar, or Tillie, the Jack Russell terrier from Brooklyn, New York, is no joke. Born in 1999, Tillie first showed artistic talent at 6 months old when she began scratching at a pad of paper.

With her owner's encouragement, Tillamook Cheddar spent years scratching and drawing various pieces of art and even had some creations hung in galleries around New York City. But even dogs have their critics in the art world! Some question whether her creations are really works of art and how much a role her owner played in her work. Tillie created **abstract art** for 15 years and died in 2014.

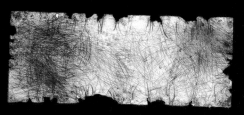

ART BY TILLAMOOK CHEDDAR

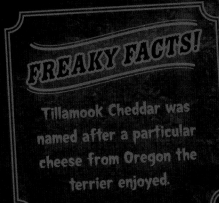

FREAKY FACTS!

Tillamook Cheddar was named after a particular cheese from Oregon the terrier enjoyed.

ANIMAL ARTISTS

Many different animals have become artists over the years. One of the most well-known animal artists was Congo, a chimpanzee who learned how to paint and draw in the 1950s and 1960s. Between the ages of two and four, Congo created nearly 400 drawings and paintings. At an auction in 2005, three of Congo's paintings sold together for $26,000, while art created by famous artists at the same auction went unsold.

THE WONDER CHICKEN

Mike was a chicken that had its head cut off by a Fruita, Colorado, farmer in 1945. Instead of becoming dinner, Mike hopped back up off the ground without his head! Mike even pecked at the ground for food.

The farmer took Mike to the University of Utah in Salt Lake City, where scientists studied Mike to figure out why he stayed alive. The ax missed his brain stem and his left ear, which meant Mike could still think and move. A blood **clot** also kept him from bleeding to **death**. Mike traveled the country on tour for more than a year as the "Headless Wonder Chicken!" His head—which the farmer had kept—even got to go with him!

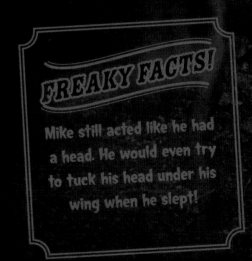

FREAKY FACTS!

Mike still acted like he had a head. He would even try to tuck his head under his wing when he slept!

FEEDING A HEADLESS CHICKEN

Mike was fed grain and water with an eyedropper to keep him alive. He actually gained weight after his head was cut off, going from 2.5 pounds (1.1 kg) to nearly 8 pounds (3.6 kg) before he died. The eyedropper—which was also used to keep his neck hole clear of mucus and food—couldn't be found in time one day in 1947. That's when Mike choked to death.

MIKE THE HEADLESS CHICKEN LIVED FOR 18 MONTHS BEFORE HE CHOKED TO DEATH IN 1947.

THE DODO BIRD

Many of the weird-looking animals that have lived on Earth have already gone extinct. The flightless dodo bird is one such animal. It lived on the island of Mauritius, in the Indian Ocean east of Madagascar. Scientists believe the bird stood over 3 feet (0.9 m) tall and weighed between 30 and 50 pounds (13.6 and 22.7 kg). Because it became extinct before cameras were invented, **accurate** images of the dodo are hard to find.

Portuguese sailors found the island in 1507, and Dutch sailors wrote about the bird in 1598. Because of overhunting by sailors, animals, and other **invasive species**, the dodo population quickly declined. The bird was last seen in 1662.

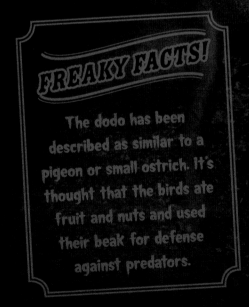

FREAKY FACTS!

The dodo has been described as similar to a pigeon or small ostrich. It's thought that the birds ate fruit and nuts and used their beak for defense against predators.

SOME THOUGHT THE DODO WAS A MYTHICAL CREATURE BECAUSE THERE WASN'T MUCH KNOWN ABOUT IT OUTSIDE OF SAILORS' STORIES.

EXTINCTION

The end of the dodo, which went extinct less than a century after discovery, brought attention to the dangers animals face from people and invasive animals. For instance, not only did sailors hunt and eat the bird, but dogs, pigs, and rats were allowed to eat the bird's eggs, eliminating the chance for reproduction. No one is certain what caused the dodo to become extinct, but because of its extinction, we now have things like endangered species lists to keep animals alive on the planet.

MAMMOTH MOVEMENT

Imagine seeing large, hairy elephants with huge tusks roaming around. If you were born 15,000 years ago, you might have seen just that. The woolly mammoth was a large ancient relative of modern-day elephants. Its large tusks were replaced six times during its lifetime! It roamed Earth, interacting with early humans who hunted the massive mammals. A combination of hunting, loss of habitat, and the last ice age, or quick cooling of Earth, all played a role in the animal's extinction.

Woolly mammoths and other ancient animals like the saber-toothed cat helped scientists learn one of the freakiest things about all life on Earth. Animals evolved, or changed over time, to adapt for survival. People have evolved, too! Maybe that means we're all freaky animals!

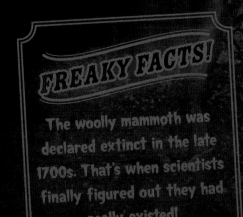

FREAKY FACTS!

The woolly mammoth was declared extinct in the late 1700s. That's when scientists finally figured out they had really existed!

MASTODON

MAMMOTH

ASIAN ELEPHANT

PALAEOMASTODON

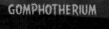

GOMPHOTHERIUM

AFRICAN ELEPHANT

SABER-TOOTHED CAT

The woolly mammoth shared Earth with lion-sized cats with large, razor-sharp teeth called saber-toothed cats. Sometimes called saber-toothed tigers, they hunted large mammals like woolly mammoths and became extinct around the same time. The introduction of people as competitive hunters may have played a part in the cats' decline, along with climate change. Being alive back then sounds freaky!

GLOSSARY

abstract art: works of art that are difficult to understand

accurate: correct or exact

conservation: the care of the natural world

duplicate: to make a copy of

endangered: in danger of dying out

genetic mutation: a change or alteration relating to or produced by genes

habitat: the natural place where an animal or plant lives

interspecies: existing or occurring between species

invasive species: one kind of living thing likely to spread and be harmful when placed in a new area

nocturnal: active at night

poacher: someone who hunts unlawfully

sensory: of or relating to the senses or sensation

FOR MORE INFORMATION

BOOKS

Berger, Melvin, and Gilda Berger. *101 Freaky Animals*. New York, NY: Scholastic, 2010.

Seuling, Barbara. *Cows Sweat Through Their Noses: And Other Freaky Facts About Animal Habits, Characteristics, and Homes.* Mankato, MN: Picture Window Books, 2008.

WEBSITES

10 Freaky Animals You Have to See to Believe
huffingtonpost.com/lucy-cooke/weird-animals_b_1676125.html
Find some pictures of more freaky animals here.

Top 10 Animal Oddities
animalplanet.com/tv-shows/weird-true-and-freaky/videos/animal-oddities/
For even more freaky fun, check out Animal Planet's top 10 freaky animals.

INDEX